PAOLO BEN SALMI aka Pint Size Adventurer

TREE TROOPS

–

LET'S EXPLORE THE TREE TROOPS FOREST

With

PAOLO BEN SALMI AKA PINT SIZE
ADVENTURER & FORESTNATION

PAOLO BEN SALMI aka Pint Size Adventurer

DEDICATION

I dedicate this book to you the reader as there is a seed inside of you and I would like to help you expand that seed through this book.

ACKNOWLEDGMENTS

I would like to take this opportunity to thank those who have always seen the best in me.

JOHN OAK "THE HIGHLY INTELLIGENT GUIDE."

"Hey there, my fellow human, I'm John Oak the great, the leader of the Tree Troops, and not to mention a handsome guy too, but anyway as you might know, I am a tree and a lot of the time you humans, yes you! Only look at the result of a seed which turns into a tree. But never seem to wonder where a tree's journey started well, I'm going to be your guide, teacher whatever you want to call me, well I'm going to take you on a tree troop journey. So, sit back on your comfy wooden chair which was probably my brother or sister from another seedling nursery, wait one second as I think about it John Olman was really busy making us, but to get to the point I John Oak The Great will be taking you on a tree troop journey.

Hello are you ready?.......... Hello! Anonymous human never mind... My cousin failure was right humans hearing is as hard as wood.

REFORESTATION WITH ForestNation

What is ForestNation and what is ForestNation's focus?

John oak Said

ForestNation Replied:

"ForestNation is a for-profit sustainable business. They offer products and services that unite environmental, social, and commercial goals together. Our focus is to empower many individuals and organizations to reforest the planet and reconnect to nature."

Wow. What is it that makes ForestNation unique from all the other reforestation companies? John said excitedly

ForestNation REPLIED:

"Our 'YOU PLANT WE PLANT' programme is what makes us unique where every item purchased on our website, we plant trees in an area hit hard by deforestation and industrial agriculture. Through this program we focus on generating sustainable livelihoods in developing countries.

Our hope is to stimulate local economies: develop leadership roles for women; and create a brighter outlook for future generations. By default, organizations that work with us help not only their own communities but contribute significantly to the greater good."

What workshops does ForestNation do in schools for kids about the environment?

John Oak asked

ForestNation Replied:

"We're planting teachable moment seeds into school fundraisers by giving educators and parents a tangible way to help kids learn about the environment. While raising money, the students will also arise awareness about the importance of caring for Mother Earth and build community in the process."

Where does ForestNation plant?

John Oak asked curiously

ForestNation Replied:

At Forestnation we plant in areas that have been affected due to deforestation, so we have planted in:

1. HAITI/MOUNTAINS OF HAITI

&

2. TANZANIA

Who in the world founded this awesome movement?

John asked excitedly

ForestNation Replied:

"Andrew Pothecary is the founder of ForestNation and has a burning desire to become successful from creating goodness that positively impacts his community, society, and mother earth.

Andrew founded ForesNation in September 2007. He has left the conception, creation, design, and everyone to grow and plant their own trees. Andrew attended kings' college university in London where he studied philosophy, and his greatest piece of advice came from a professor named mark Sainsbury; "whatever it is you do in life make sure it has purpose."

Andrew believes that planting trees will make the planet healthy, so it can provide us with everything we need. If we all adopt the custom of growing our own trees and giving back to earth on a regular basis it will bring about a change in us. It will even connect us all with each other.

This is awesome! I also wanted to ask, how can gardening help fight climate change?

ForestNation Replied:

"One of the most helpful things that you can do for the environment is to grow your own herb garden or vegetable patch. Not only does it mean fresh, organic produce all year round, but herbs can also help boost your energy and motivation. It also allows you to reduce your carbon footprint, as everything you consume won't need to travel far to reach you.

WOW I Might start gardening myself I didn't know that a simple act of gardening can have a huge impact in the environment we live in. Learning this, it made me wonder; How can gardening help clean the air and the ground in the most natural way?

John said at the edge of his chair.

ForestNation Replied:

"Looking after your garden can be a wonderful, all-natural way to maintain the air and the solid clean. In fact, plants generate oxygen through a process called photosynthesis, in which they take carbon dioxide from the atmosphere and use it to eliminate water and oxygen."

"In addition to this, the plants then get rid of potentially dangerous chemicals and bacteria that are often present in the air, thus creating an even cleaner environment."

Does that mean that when you don't maintain your garden, it's likely, that you are releasing bacteria both in the soil and in the air?

ForestNation Replied:

Yes evidently, so, anyone with a garden what you must do is take care of it because it affects the planet and even the air that they breathe in at home.

Wow I really need to act as my garden is looking a bit like Albert Einstein's hair, I also wanted to ask.

How can we all create a safe environment for important insects and animals?

ForestNation Replied:

"Certain species of insects and animals are very precious for our planet, but unfortunately, many of these are at risk of extinction. By growing your own garden, you can do your bit to help protect these super-important creatures.

We are mostly referring. To insects like bees, and animals like birds. Bees are absolutely vital to the process of pollination, whereas birds contribute to keeping unwanted bugs at bay, as well as spreading seeds. Your garden can become a safe little haven to help protect these vital species and, ultimately, the planet."

Wow I now understand how important most insects and animals are to our world. How can gardening help nurture the soil?

John asked

ForestNation Replied

"Gardening can help nurture the soil. This happens because the roots of your plants help to bind the soil underneath them, protecting them, protecting it and nourishing it.

In order to maximize this, you're going to need to know what exactly you should plant and when."

What does ForestNation educate villages on, in Haiti requesting reforestation?

John asked

ForestNation Replied:

1. Education

ForestNation Educates them on:

- Where and how to plant each kind of tree

- What trees provide to the ecosystem and to the people

- Compositing

- Companion planting with crops, shade grown crops ect

- How to best stop goats from eating the seedlings

2. Fruit Tree Distribution

After the seminar everyone receives a few fruit trees like mango or lemon that we know people value greatly since they each cost around $3 USD to purchase.

We visit lots of villages and educate and distribute a few fruit trees to everyone who comes to the seminar, and in return, we find a few great people willing to tirelessly reforest mountainsides because they have the same vision of Haiti that we do.

3. Start Tree Nurseries

If a village seems eager and organized enough to start a tree nursery, we provide the training and costs for the first season of tree planting. People in the community take the trees home to plant them.

Farmers select the tree species they want to grow and plant; they own the trees, and they are responsible for caring for them. Prior to even starting a tree nursery we conduct a needs assessment with community or individual farmer to determine what species they would like to use and how best to plant them.

4. A Tree Planting Culture Is Born

Our efforts move on to another village leaving precious villages hungry for more trees to plant. §§ villages who received the aide soon realize that they can grow trees on their own without help. It takes some resourcefulness and teamwork. As a result, a culture of planting trees is born.

HERE ARE SOME STATS ON THE TREE PLANTING IN HAITI FROM MONDAY 13 OF SEPTEMBER 2021 AT 12:56pm.

29,519
Trees have been planted it Haiti so far and that number is yet to enlarge.

And those trees create a total of
737.975

Tons of CO_2 absorbed per year
Which then creates a total of

2,951.9

Tons of O_2 created per year

Which leaves

1,180.76
work hours created per year

creating a total of

29.519
Hectares of land restored

Visit the website to see up to date data:
https://forestnation.com/blog/haiti-project/

ACTIVITIES

QUIZ: 1

WHO IS THE FOUNDER OF FOREST NATION?

Circle the correct answer

a. **Andrew Pothen**

b. **Andrew Pite**

c. **Andrew Pothecary**

QUIZ: 2

HOW MANY TREES WERE PLANTED IN HAITI?

Circle the correct answer

a. 20,00

b. 29,519

c. 29,000,000

QUIZ: 3

WHERE DOES FORESTNATION PLANT TREES

Circle the correct answer

1. HAITI

2. TANZANIA

3. OR BOTH

QUIZ ANSWERS

QUIZ: 1
ANSWER

ANSWER: C - Andrew Pothcary

QUIZ: 2
ANSWER

ANSWER: B - 29,519

QUIZ: 3
ANSWER

ANSWER: 3 - BOTH

How will you contribute to reforestation?

I will contribute to reforestation by_____

_____

_____

_____

_____

_____

_____

_____

_____

_____

_____

_____

_____

_____

_____

_____

_____

_____

_____

_____

_____

_____

_____

8 FACTS ABOUT PAOLO

1. PAOLO HAS PLANTED 10,00 TREES IN TANZANIA IN PARTNERSHIP WITH BORG INVESTMENT BANK

2. PAOLO IS 12 YEARS OLD

3. PAOLO HAS 4 OTHER SIBLINGS

4. PAOLO LOVES TREES

5. PAOLO HAS WRITTEN OVER 6 BOOKS

6. PAOLO IS A CLIMATE CHANGE ACTIVIST

7. PAOLO LOVES PIZZA

8. PAOLO HAS A PODCAST CALLED LIFE ACCORDING TO PAOLO

STEM: LIVING THINGS | PLANT FEATURES

Inquiry question: How do humans use plants?

Plants not only provide people with food to eat, but also serve other equally important functions. For example, plants:

- Provide shelter for animals
- Are a source of food for other animals
- Provide oxygen to maintain the atmosphere
- Produce products such as firewood, medicines, timber, oil, rubbers and so on.

Instructions: Research and brainstorm below, all the different uses for plants, using specific examples for each.

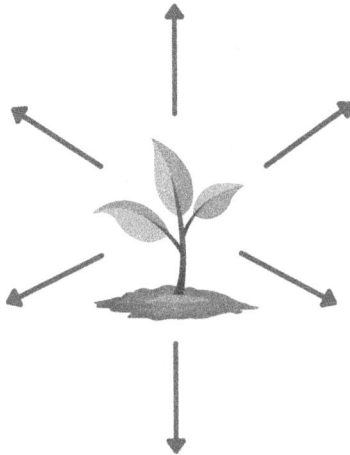

NATIONAL TREE DAY

PLANT A TREE: SUNDAY 1ST AUGUST

Find-a-word

TREES

P	E	T	R	N	G	N	I	V	I	L
L	G	R	O	W	N	U	T	S	A	L
A	R	E	R	G	M	R	S	F	U	L
N	T	E	T	W	I	G	S	N	S	L
T	A	A	Z	S	I	S	G	E	E	I
S	T	T	O	H	N	S	T	K	H	O
F	O	L	I	A	G	E	R	R	C	S
B	R	L	T	R	U	N	K	A	N	D
R	I	O	H	O	M	E	T	B	A	E
D	O	X	Y	G	E	N	O	T	R	E
R	T	I	M	B	E	R	I	A	B	S

Instructions: Find the underlined words in the above find-a-word.

Trees are living things. They are plants that grow from seeds. The structure of a tree includes a root system, trunk, branches, twigs and a crown of foliage. Trees are regarded as the lungs of earth, filtering out dust and converting carbon dioxide into oxygen. They are also the home to many animals, provide shelter to human, timber for construction and edible fruits, nuts, seeds, flowers and even bark.

My Family Tree

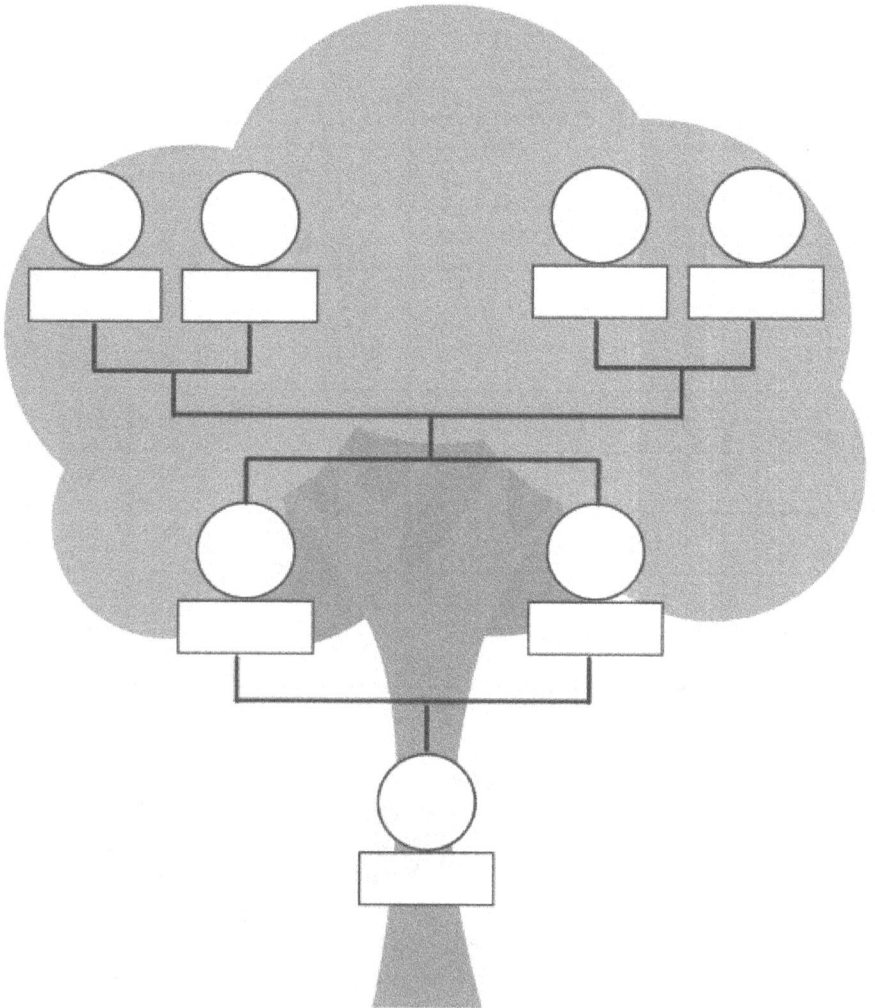

Photosynthesis

Photosynthesis is the process where plants transform light energy into chemical energy. Plants use this energy to make their own food. The light energy they captured is used to convert carbon dioxide, water, and minerals into oxygen.

Chlorophyll

The pigment that gives plants their green color and helps in the process of photosynthesis.

Did you know?

There are organisms other than plants that can undergo photosynthesis. These include algae and the emerald green sea slug.

The Photosynthesis Process

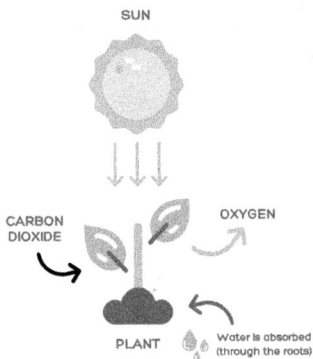

SUN

CARBON DIOXIDE

OXYGEN

PLANT

Water is absorbed (through the roots)

Plants take in water and carbon dioxide and use energy from the sun to turn them into food.

Within the plant cell, water is oxidized, loses electrons, and is changed into oxygen. Carbon dioxide is reduced, gains electrons, and turns into glucose.

Oxygen is released, and glucose is stored within the plant as energy.

The Photosynthesis Formula

$$6CO_2 + 6H_2O \longrightarrow C_6H_{12}O_6 + 6O_2$$

CARBON DIOXIDE   WATER   SUGAR   OXYGEN

Sources: Encyclopedia Britannica & National Geographic.

PLANT A
SEED
JOURNAL

PLANT A SEED JOURNAL

Writing things down is an effective way to help you to remember and reflect on all the amazing things that happen every day. Please use this 'Plant Your Seed Journal' to start and end your day in an uplifting and positive way.

No matter how much you write or how little you write take the time to really think about your day, at the end of your journal you can then go back and treasure those memories

Date: __/__/____ Today I am Grateful For…

_____

_____

_____

What Would Make Today A Great Day?

_____

_____

_____

During the evening just before going to bed take a moment to reflect on your day then List the 3 best things that happened…

1) _____

_____

2) _____

_____

3) _____

_____

Date: __/__/____ Today I am Grateful For...

_____

_____

_____

What Would Make Today A Great Day?

_____

_____

_____

During the evening just before going to bed take a moment to reflect on your day then List the 3 best things that happened...

1) _____

_____

2) _____

_____

3) _____

_____

Date: __/__/____ Today I am Grateful For…

_____

_____

_____

What Would Make Today A Great Day?

_____

_____

_____

During the evening just before going to bed take a moment to reflect on your day then List the 3 best things that happened…

1) _____

_____

2) _____

_____

3) _____

_____

Date: __/__/____ Today I am Grateful For...

_____

_____

_____

What Would Make Today A Great Day?

_____

_____

_____

During the evening just before going to bed take a moment to reflect on your day then List the 3 best things that happened...

1) _____

   _____

2) _____

   _____

3) _____

   _____

Date: __/__/____ Today I am Grateful For...

_____

_____

_____

What Would Make Today A Great Day?

_____

_____

_____

During the evening just before going to bed take a moment to reflect on your day then List the 3 best things that happened...

1) _____

_____

2) _____

_____

3) _____

_____

Date: __/__/____ Today I am Grateful For...

_____

_____

_____

What Would Make Today A Great Day?

_____

_____

_____

During the evening just before going to bed take a moment to reflect on your day then List the 3 best things that happened...

1) _____

_____

2) _____

_____

3) _____

_____

Date: __/__/____ Today I am Grateful For...

_____

_____

_____

What Would Make Today A Great Day?

_____

_____

_____

During the evening just before going to bed take a moment to reflect on your day then List the 3 best things that happened...

1) _____

_____

2) _____

_____

3) _____

_____

Date: __/__/____ Today I am Grateful For...

_____

_____

_____

What Would Make Today A Great Day?

_____

_____

_____

During the evening just before going to bed take a moment to reflect on your day then List the 3 best things that happened...

1) _____

_____

2) _____

_____

3) _____

_____

Date: __/__/____ Today I am Grateful For...

_____

_____

_____

What Would Make Today A Great Day?

_____

_____

_____

During the evening just before going to bed take a moment to reflect on your day then List the 3 best things that happened...

1) _____

_____

2) _____

_____

3) _____

_____

Date: __/__/____ Today I am Grateful For...

_____

_____

_____

What Would Make Today A Great Day?

_____

_____

_____

During the evening just before going to bed take a moment to reflect on your day then List the 3 best things that happened...

1) _____

_____

2) _____

_____

3) _____

_____

Date: __/__/____ Today I am Grateful For...

_____

_____

_____

What Would Make Today A Great Day?

_____

_____

_____

During the evening just before going to bed take a moment to reflect on your day then List the 3 best things that happened...

1) _____

_____

2) _____

_____

3) _____

_____

Date: __/__/____ Today I am Grateful For...

_____

_____

_____

What Would Make Today A Great Day?

_____

_____

_____

During the evening just before going to bed take a moment to reflect on your day then List the 3 best things that happened...

1) _____

_____

2) _____

_____

3) _____

_____

Date: __/__/____ Today I am Grateful For...

_____

_____

_____

What Would Make Today A Great Day?

_____

_____

_____

During the evening just before going to bed take a moment to reflect on your day then List the 3 best things that happened...

1) _____

_____

2) _____

_____

3) _____

_____

Date: __/__/____ Today I am Grateful For...

_____

_____

_____

What Would Make Today A Great Day?

_____

_____

_____

During the evening just before going to bed take a moment to reflect on your day then List the 3 best things that happened...

1) _____

_____

2) _____

_____

3) _____

_____

Date: __/__/____ Today I am Grateful For...

_____

_____

_____

What Would Make Today A Great Day?

_____

_____

_____

During the evening just before going to bed take a moment to reflect on your day then List the 3 best things that happened...

1) _____

_____

2) _____

_____

3) _____

_____

Date: __/__/____ Today I am Grateful For...

_____

_____

_____

What Would Make Today A Great Day?

_____

_____

_____

During the evening just before going to bed take a moment to reflect on your day then List the 3 best things that happened...

1) _____

_____

2) _____

_____

3) _____

_____

Date: __/__/____ Today I am Grateful For...

_____

_____

_____

What Would Make Today A Great Day?

_____

_____

_____

During the evening just before going to bed take a moment to reflect on your day then List the 3 best things that happened...

1) _____

_____

2) _____

_____

3) _____

_____

Date: __/__/____ Today I am Grateful For...

_____

_____

_____

What Would Make Today A Great Day?

_____

_____

_____

During the evening just before going to bed take a moment to reflect on your day then List the 3 best things that happened...

1) _____

_____

2) _____

_____

3) _____

_____

Date: __/__/____ Today I am Grateful For...

_____

_____

_____

What Would Make Today A Great Day?

_____

_____

_____

During the evening just before going to bed take a moment to reflect on your day then List the 3 best things that happened...

1) _____

_____

2) _____

_____

3) _____

_____

Date: __/__/____ Today I am Grateful For...

_____

_____

_____

What Would Make Today A Great Day?

_____

_____

_____

During the evening just before going to bed take a moment to reflect on your day then List the 3 best things that happened...

1) _____

_____

2) _____

_____

3) _____

_____

Date: __/__/____ Today I am Grateful For...

_____

_____

_____

What Would Make Today A Great Day?

_____

_____

_____

During the evening just before going to bed take a moment to reflect on your day then List the 3 best things that happened...

1) _____

_____

2) _____

_____

3) _____

_____

Date: __/__/____ Today I am Grateful For…

_____

_____

_____

What Would Make Today A Great Day?

_____

_____

_____

During the evening just before going to bed take a moment to reflect on your day then List the 3 best things that happened…

1) _____

_____

2) _____

_____

3) _____

_____

Date: __/__/____ Today I am Grateful For...

_____

_____

_____

What Would Make Today A Great Day?

_____

_____

_____

During the evening just before going to bed take a moment to reflect on your day then List the 3 best things that happened...

1) _____

_____

2) _____

_____

3) _____

_____

Date: __/__/____ Today I am Grateful For...

_____

_____

_____

What Would Make Today A Great Day?

_____

_____

_____

During the evening just before going to bed take a moment to reflect on your day then List the 3 best things that happened...

1) _____

_____

2) _____

_____

3) _____

_____

Date: __/__/____ Today I am Grateful For...

_____

_____

_____

What Would Make Today A Great Day?

_____

_____

_____

During the evening just before going to bed take a moment to reflect on your day then List the 3 best things that happened...

1) _____

_____

2) _____

_____

3) _____

_____

Date: __/__/____ Today I am Grateful For…

_____

_____

_____

What Would Make Today A Great Day?

_____

_____

_____

During the evening just before going to bed take a moment to reflect on your day then List the 3 best things that happened…

1) _____

_____

2) _____

_____

3) _____

_____

Date: __/__/____ Today I am Grateful For…

_____

_____

_____

What Would Make Today A Great Day?

_____

_____

_____

During the evening just before going to bed take a moment to reflect on your day then List the 3 best things that happened…

1) _____

_____

2) _____

_____

3) _____

_____

Date: __/__/____ Today I am Grateful For...

_____

_____

_____

What Would Make Today A Great Day?

_____

_____

_____

During the evening just before going to bed take a moment to reflect on your day then List the 3 best things that happened...

1) _____

_____

2) _____

_____

3) _____

_____

Date: __/__/____ Today I am Grateful For...

_____

_____

_____

What Would Make Today A Great Day?

_____

_____

_____

During the evening just before going to bed take a moment to reflect on your day then List the 3 best things that happened...

1) _____

_____

2) _____

_____

3) _____

_____

Date: __/__/____ Today I am Grateful For...

_____

_____

_____

What Would Make Today A Great Day?

_____

_____

_____

During the evening just before going to bed take a moment to reflect on your day then List the 3 best things that happened...

1) _____

_____

2) _____

_____

3) _____

_____

Date: __/__/____ Today I am Grateful For...

_____

_____

_____

What Would Make Today A Great Day?

_____

_____

_____

During the evening just before going to bed take a moment to reflect on your day then List the 3 best things that happened...

1) _____

_____

2) _____

_____

3) _____

_____

Date: __/__/____ Today I am Grateful For...

_____

_____

_____

What Would Make Today A Great Day?

_____

_____

_____

During the evening just before going to bed take a moment to reflect on your day then List the 3 best things that happened...

1) _____

_____

2) _____

_____

3) _____

_____

Date: __/__/____ Today I am Grateful For...

_____

_____

_____

What Would Make Today A Great Day?

_____

_____

_____

During the evening just before going to bed take a moment to reflect on your day then List the 3 best things that happened...

1) _____

_____

2) _____

_____

3) _____

_____

Date: __/__/____ Today I am Grateful For…

_____

_____

_____

What Would Make Today A Great Day?

_____

_____

_____

During the evening just before going to bed take a moment to reflect on your day then List the 3 best things that happened…

1) _____

_____

2) _____

_____

3) _____

_____

Date: __/__/____ Today I am Grateful For...

_____

_____

_____

What Would Make Today A Great Day?

_____

_____

_____

During the evening just before going to bed take a moment to reflect on your day then List the 3 best things that happened...

1) _____

_____

2) _____

_____

3) _____

_____

ABOUT THE AUTHOR

AS HEARD ON RADIO & AS SEEN ON TV & IN NEWSPAPERS & MAGAZINES

Purpose: To inspire 1 million young people to explore their internal and external world through the teaching of self-discovery, exploration, and engineering planting one seed at a time

Websites: https://linktr.ee/AuthorPaolobensalmi

2021 Paolo was a guest speaker on for the UN (United Nations) Global Goals 2030 thanks to I AM The Code founder Lady Marieme Jamme

Podcast Show Host of Life according To Paolo: https://paolobensalmi.sounder.fm/show/life-according-to-paolo

Paolo is the youngest ever Water-to-Go Ambassador: WWW.WATERTOGO.EU/PARTNERSHIPS/PAOLOBENSALMI

Paolo is one of five siblings (21-year-old Lashai Ben Salmi, 16-year-old Tray-Sean Ben Salmi, 14-year-old Yasmine Ben Salmi and 8-year-old Amire Ben Salmi)

Paolo was chosen to develop UnLtd application process together with his mother, big brother Tray-Sean and big sister Lashai.

Paolo Ben Salmi is a 12-year-old personal development coach and founder of Pint Size Adventurer. Paolo is here to help you plant the seed toward self-discovery, exploration of the internal and external world. Paolo offers a variety of products and services to assist you to create a brighter future. His desire is to encourage as many children as possible to go on adventures both internally and externally to activate their natural curiosity.

Paolo Ben Salmi aka The Tree Whisper Fruit Forest steward in Tanzania (he planted **10,000** trees) ◢: Borg Global Holdings - Forest Nation Forests. Paolo Ben Salmi aka The Tree Whisper fruit forest steward in Tanzania ◢: Borg Global Holdings - ForestNation Forests

Brunel University London (B.U.L) has given the Ben Salmi family the opportunity to participate in Masterclasses covering Engineering, Computer Science and currently the Environmental Agency Masterclass.

Paolo's youngest brother **8**-year-old Amire is proud to be the youngest ever honorary STEM Ambassador in history for Brunel University London (B.U.L).

B.U.L has given the homeschooled families the opportunity to participate in masterclasses for the first time in history thanks to Lesley Warren.

Paolo has interviewed people like Ari Rastegar, Harry Hugo, Travis W Fox, Douglas Vermeeren, Bernardodo Mayo, Bob Doyle, Meagen Fettes, Udo Erasmus and Dr John Demartini to name a few.

Paolo Ben Salmi is an award-winning publisher and author of the book series called 'Pint Size Adventurer - **10** Keys Principles to Get Your Kids off their iPads & Into the Wild.'
Paolo is an Award-Winning public speaker, publisher, author and visionary, who has spoken at venues such as Mercedes Benz World, Chelsea FC and Virgin Money alongside his family.

My family and I have been acknowledged in the credits of a NEW movie called: How Thoughts Become Things movie promotional link:

Bit.ly/HowThoughtsBecomeThingsMovie2020

Water-to-Go blog about Paolo:
https://www.watertogo.eu/blog/meet-paolo-water-to-gos-youngest-ever-ambassador/

Paolo is the founder of his own publishing house called Adventurous Publishing.

Paolo hosted his signature program called Pint Size Adventurer - The Abundant Adventure Creator™ at the prestigious Virgin Money Lounge:
London Haymarket: Pint Size Adventurer - The Abundant Adventure Creator - My Virgin Money

Paolo Ben Salmi is an award-winning author of the book series called Pint Size Adventurer - 10 Keys Principles to Get Your KIDS off their iPads & Into the Wild.

Paolo is an Award-Winning Public Speaker (who has spoken at eleventh such as Mercedes Benz World and Virgin etc.)

Paolo has participated in brand campaigns for Sainsburys, Legoland, Matr, Warner Bros, Sony and Made for Mums to name a few.

Thanks to Douglas Vermeeren back in **2017** Paolo made history by being the youngest to interview Dr. John Demartini:
https://www.facebook.com/350400542063654/videos/363072487463126/

Paolo desires to encourage as many children as possible to go on adventures both internally and externally to activate their natural curiosity.

The question is are you watching the movie, in the movie or directing the movie?

Book:

PINT SIZE ADVENTURER - How to Become An Author Using 7 Key Principles
https://www.amazon.co.uk/dp/1913310191/ref=cm_s w_r_cp_api_fabc_97MRV7C3RASF7NKA4K4R

Pint Size Adventurer - Mindset Is KEY
https://www.amazon.co.uk/dp/1913310337/ref=cm_s w_r_cp_api_fabt1_.AdVFbHXR201J

Pint Sized Adventurer: The Abundant Adventure Creator
https://www.amazon.co.uk/PINT-SIZE-ADVENTURER-ABUNDANT-ADVENTURE/dp/1913310183/ref=tmm_pap_swatch_0?_encoding=UTF8&qid=1585959464&sr=1-1

TREE TROOPS: AN EPIC ADVENTURE OF DISCOVERY
https://www.amazon.co.uk/dp/1913310612/ref=cm_s w_r_cp_api_glt_fabc_Q6FMV25GHXEPT0WJ5VF9

Facebook page Pint Size Adventurer:
https://m.facebook.com/paolobensalmiakapintsize adventurer/

BEN SALMI FAMILY MANTRA

"BEN SALMI TEAMWORK MAKES THE DREAMWORK

We believe that there is no such thing as failure only feedback.

We also believe that the journey of one thousand miles begins with a single step in the right direction

FAMILY ANTHEM

If you want to be somebody,
If you want to go somewhere,
You better wake up and PAY
ATTENTION

I'm ready to be somebody,
I'm ready to go somewhere,
I'm ready to wake up and PAY
ATTENTION!

The question is **ARE YOU?**

COME PLANT A TREE WITH US IN OUR TREE TROOPS FOREST

We would like you to know that we plant a tree to promote permaculture in Haiti in our very own Tree Troops Forest with our partner ForestNation. This will help reforestation on our planet and create sustainable livelihoods for people in Haiti.

Thanks for making an impact!
USE THIS LINK TO PLANT A TREE IN OUR TREE TROOPS FOREST:
https://forestnation.com/net/forests/treetroops/